TAKE BACK
THE WHEEL

TAKE BACK THE WHEEL

How to Help Make Your Teenager's High School Journey Successful

Betty J. McGee

iUniverse, Inc.
Bloomington

Take Back The Wheel
How to Help Make Your Teenager's High School Journey Successful

iUniverse books may be ordered through booksellers or by contacting:

iUniverse
1663 Liberty Drive
Bloomington, IN 47403
www.iuniverse.com
1-800-Authors (1-800-288-4677)

Because of the dynamic nature of the Internet, any Web addresses or links contained in this book may have changed since publication and may no longer be valid. The views expressed in this work are solely those of the author and do not necessarily reflect the views of the publisher, and the publisher hereby disclaims any responsibility for them.

ISBN: 978-0-5952-3620-6 (sc)

Printed in the United States of America

iUniverse rev. date: 06/16/2011

To my mom: You did your best and it was good enough.

Behind every successful high school student is an involved parent.

Contents

List of Tables

Acknowledgments

I acknowledge each of you with joy and gratitude:

Thank you *Karen Collins, Elva Gabriel,* **and** *Bill Gonsalves* for recommending me for the job of Outreach Consultant at Oakland Technical High School. The work that I did helped me realize what I am most passionate about in life.

Thank you principals *Christine Dargahi and Larry Todd,* for allowing me to be a creative worker and supporting my vision about parent involvement at the high school level. It was a pleasure working with the two of you.

Thank you *Oakland Technical High Schools Staff and Community,* for supporting my work. Your support made a difference in the lives of many students and their parents.

Thank you *Pamela Wright,* for being the wonderful parent that you are. Parenting is hard work. You made it known to everyone that being a single parent would not get in the way of making sure your sons complete their basic education. You met every teacher, counselor, principal, and vice principal. It was a joy and a delight working with you, and I learned a lot. Parents and educators can work together; it is not a mission impossible.

Thank you Marco Orlando and Claire Paul, for giving me an audience to speak from my heart about the importance of parent involvement at the high school level. For nearly a decade I have enjoyed sharing my knowledge with parents and educators at the Annual California Dropout Prevention Conference.

A special thanks to *Edward,* my spouse, dearest friend, and anchor in life. Thank you for the amount of time and energy you put into editing every page of ***Take Back the Wheel.***

Introduction

Dear Parent (*a.k.a.* Primary Teacher and Elder):

The two questions that I am asked most often by parents of students who are failing in high school are: 1. Can you put my child in the right grade? 2. If my child is not on track to graduate, what are the options? These kinds of questions suggest to me that parents need to be involved in their child's education at the high school level. What do you think?

How would you define the importance of working in close partnership with teachers during your child's high school years?

1. Not necessary, the teachers and the students will do fine.
2. It would be nice, if it could be worked out.
3. Critical!

Unfortunately, if you answered #1 or #2, what you don't know about the benefits of parents and teachers working in concert at this level can hurt your teenager in more ways than you think. Consider the following situations:

Situation #1

Your son is a senior in high school and has many accomplishments to his credit, including a term as class president during his sophomore year and two consecutive years as a star athlete. His graduation day is much anticipated by your family and friends. But you unexpectedly receive a letter from your son's counselor, and the news is not good: your son will not be graduating! He is two credits shy of what is needed for his diploma. How could this have happened, and why didn't you know?

Situation #2

Your freshman daughter has failed three of her six fall semester classes. Then, in the spring semester, her math and English teachers have each said that they can no longer tolerate your daughter's rude and disruptive behavior. Both teachers have requested that she be dropped from their class. However, there are no alternative classes available for her to enroll in. Without the classes, your daughter will not earn enough credits for promotion to the next grade level, even if she attends summer school! What went wrong?

Working as an Outreach Consultant within a public high school for over 13 years, I have personally witnessed many teenagers dropping out of high school for a variety of reasons. According to the National Center for Education Statistics (October 1999), approximately 3.8 million young adults, or 11.2 percent of all 16- through 24-year-olds in the United States, were not enrolled in a high school program and had not completed high school (status dropouts). I have also seen many students being allowed to graduate with below-average academic and social skills.

Coinciding with this, I have watched the thrill of imparting knowledge and challenging young minds fade for many individuals working in education.

Who is at fault concerning our children's education? Who is responsible for teenagers failing in our public high schools? Is it parents, teachers, administrators, or students? And what is the solution?

It seems that everyone has an opinion about who is at fault, yet unfortunately there appears to be little or no commitment from individuals to band together to find a way to resolve this dilemma collectively.

Having been a part of many conversations regarding the problems in public education at the secondary level, I find that a few consistent themes emerge from concerned members of various involved groups.

The Parents Speak Out:

"Our children are failing; they are not being motivated to learn. When there is a problem, the teachers don't notify us until it's too late! And when we are contacted, they come across as intimidating and we are made to feel uncomfortable. They expect too much from us; why can't they handle their end?"

The Teachers Sound Off:

"Our students are failing because the parents are not paying attention to their children's educational needs. Too many parents behave as if they do not know what the situation is. They expect us to help raise their children. Our job is to educate, not to raise, the students. And many students just want to be given grades without earning them."

"Most of our administrators do not support us. They are opportunists. They just want more money, they don't have to work in the classroom, and they flaunt their title of being "the boss."

The Administrators Weigh in:

"Our students are failing because parents and teachers are not working as a team. They are very capable of working together, and we support them in this effort. But on our end, we also are trying to address other pressing issues as well, such as school safety, student achievement, attendance and disciplinary problems, etc."

And finally,

The Students Say:

"We are failing because many of our teachers do not like us and they can't teach. High school is boring and it is not relevant."

Personally, I do not feel that any one group is completely at fault. However, I do believe that parents, students, teachers, and administrators all share the blame for this awful mess. It seems as if much of it has to do with the ill feelings and misperceptions between the groups. These feelings and misperceptions prevent us from moving forward and succeeding in our work.

Arguing our issues and feelings is fine when we have a plan to resolve our concerns. A plan that must begin with: Eliminate the blame! To blame one another is not resolving our problems; it is what everyone is willing to do that will solve problems.

Take Back the Wheel is about how to make your teenager's high school journey successful. It is about the many paths that you must travel in order to help your child succeed in his final stage of the K-through-12 program. This guidebook looks at some of the most common parental failings as they may relate to your child's high school progress. These mistakes may be unintentional, but they might also be viewed as gross acts of negligence.

Take Back the Wheel delves into how to give your teenager a healthy start as a high school student. This is the beginning of the journey. It is about preventing acts of negligence that can victimize your child when you are unaware of what you need to do.

Take Back the Wheel addresses what you need to do to be mindful. This means recognizing your duties and responsibilities, and having the courage to do what is necessary. What you are mindful of will help you communicate more effectively with teachers. It will help you understand the role that you must play in your child's education. This guidebook illuminates what many public high school teachers mean when they say, "We want parents to become more actively involved."

And finally, *Take Back the Wheel* is about how you can handle the pain and the frustrations that can occur as the parent of a failing high school student. It offers a few simple solutions to help you manage many of the heartaches and disappointments that arise when things seem to be off course. It addresses how to continue the journey no matter how tired and frustrated you have become. There are a few heartfelt observations that suggest why you need to be more actively involved in your child's high school education, and why it is imperative that you enlist the involvement of other parents and elders. It offers information about interventions — getting help for your child and for yourself.

In summary, *Take Back the Wheel* is for parents who:

- Are about to enroll their teenager in a public high school.
- Need to raise their awareness of the choices they have for being involved.
- Feel that they do not have the time to become active in their child's education.

- Feel that they should limit their involvement in the education process now that their child is in high school.
- Are currently experiencing "the Blues" because their teenager is failing in high school.

It is my hope that you will find this guidebook informative and practical. It is my desire that my suggestions will stimulate you to move beyond any negative feelings and perceptions you may have toward public high school educators; and it is my dream that you will find this information worth passing on. The messages in this book will serve as a reminder that parents and educators do have common goals. And as such, you have the freedom to determine how you would like to work together. But remember, when you make your choice, you are committing to being accountable. I wish you a successful journey in your efforts to help your teenager reach success.

Good luck!
Betty J. McGee
Teacher/Outreach Worker/Community Consultant/Elder

Chapter One

You've Got the Blues...
the High School Blues

"If there's a single message passed down from each generation of American parents to their children, it is a two-word line: Better Yourself. And if there's a temple of self-betterment in each town, it is the local school. We have worshipped there for some time."

— Ellen Goodman

Let's take a look at a number of situations and circumstances by which many parents suddenly find themselves overwhelmed. Either specifically or generally, maybe they are familiar to you.

***

What Went Wrong?

In his growing years, you took many opportunities to impress your child with the importance of an education, and what life would be like without it. You raised your child to be respectful to adults, and you often tell friends and family how smart and caring he is. You reflect with pride about your child, but recently his lack of success and his behavior in high school are very disturbing to you.

Your child's teachers and other school personnel have been contacting you with calls and letters. You are unfamiliar with some of these people. They are telling you things about your child, that are unflattering-and in some instances shocking. For example:

BEHAVIOR

The behavior of your child is unacceptable at school. He is rude toward the teachers and other staff members; he refuses to do classwork or homework. He is not getting along with his peers. You knew that your child's behavior was erratic at home, but you hoped that things were different at school.

GRADES

Your child's grades have fallen dramatically. You are stunned because your child was a high achiever before entering high school.

ATTENDANCE

Your child is chronically a truant. You had no idea that he was not attending classes. You are surprised! You ask your child every day, "How was school?" and his response is always, "It was fine."

When your child does go to school, he is not attending many of his classes. Some of his teachers have not even met him. He roams the halls and socializes with other students who also are not attending class. You are having a hard time accepting this information. You don't understand! You send your child to school every day. All of his teachers should know him! He is there to learn, not just to socialize!

PROGRESS

- Your child will be repeating the ninth grade. You knew that your child was having problems, but you had no idea how extreme things had become.

- Your child will not be graduating. You knew that your child had failed several classes, but you were under the impression that he had made up the work by attending summer school. You are confused.

But that is only part of your picture of concerns. School officials now have several demands of you.

THEY ASK

- Get your child to school, attending class; then,

- Make your child behave appropriately or consider enrolling him in another school.

So there we have it. Your teenager is "at risk" of failing to complete his basic education. This is not something that you had anticipated. You had heard about the pain and the frustrations of many parents because of their child's failure to complete school. However, you never thought that this could happen to you. You are embarrassed about what is going on with your child, and you are worried what friends, teachers, and others might be thinking. You may even wonder:

- Did you do your best to help your child understand the importance of an education?

- Did you do your best to raise a well-behaved child?

- Are you a good parent?

As the parent of an unsuccessful student, you are concerned. You are having a hard time coping with "the Blues", feeling overwhelmed and exhausted.

- You are overwhelmed because you have the most challenging and important job in the world: being a parent. More is expected from parents than from people in any other roles. You know that you must do something to help your child, but you are not sure exactly what it is.

- You are exhausted, too, because being a parent is not your only job. Yet so many people look to you to do everything well. And sometimes others won't recognize that you are doing your best. You are doing what you know. You can <u>only</u> do what you know!

- You have observations and feelings about a number of things in this situation. You are disappointed in some of the teachers and the format of secondary education. You vaguely (or definitely!) sense that no one is willing or able to help your child.

It may seem that your child's school setting presents or perpetuates the following circumstances:

- Your child is frustrated and, as a result, unhappy with his or her task of learning. Your child may, at the same time, be placed in classrooms with teachers who are equally frustrated and unhappy with their task of teaching—for any number of reasons. Your concern: Your child is not in an environment conducive to learning.

- Some teachers do not have sufficiently high expectations of your child.

- Some teachers may not be proficient in the subjects they are teaching.

- Several teachers feel that in fairness to the students who are serious about learning, and for the sake of their sanity, they must focus on the students who are well behaved and are willing to learn. As things stand, *this obviously leaves your child out.*

- Teaching and learning in the classroom stops when there is a substitute teacher. *You are concerned that substitute teachers are not being viewed as "real" teachers, but rather as baby-sitters.*

So you have concerns about what teachers and other school officials are saying in regard to your child and how they may perceive you as a parent. But you also note your observations and concerns, asking yourself: "What can I do both to prevent and to remedy what I see?"

***

Here Is a Way

The Path of Doing (Chapter 2) and The Path of Knowing (Chapter 3) are about preventing certain problems that often arise in public education at the high school level.

As you read Chapters 2 and 3, you will:

- Be able to see what you need to do and be aware.

- Be introduced to solutions that can eliminate, or at least reduce, the number of factors that are currently giving you "the Blues."

The Path of Interventions (Chapter 4) is about getting additional help to complete the journey when you have done your best, yet your child is still not experiencing success as a high school student.

And finally, The Workbook provides you with a place to plan, to document, and to reflect, as you *Take Back the Wheel,* steering your teenager to a successful completion of the high school journey.

***

Chapter Two

The Journey Begins:
The Path of Doing

"In truth, school is a desperate duel between new souls and old to pass on facts and methods and dreams from a dying world, without letting either teacher or taught lose for a moment faith and interest. It is hard work... It is never wholly a success without the painstaking help of the parent."

—W.E.B. Du Bois

There is a widely held view that behind every successful student is an involved parent. Without the guidance of supportive parents or guardians, many students are unable to master the skills necessary for school-related success. This type of involvement in your child's life is ***The Path of Doing.***

The aim of ***The Path of Doing*** is to help parents of public high school students avoid common errors that they can frequently make. It provides ways to stay clear of potential problems. Hopefully, these methods will:

- Help you give your teenager a solid start as a high school student;
- Aid you in minimizing the conflicts and misunderstandings that can arise when interacting with teachers; and
- Enable you to maintain your good reputation as a parent concerned and involved in your child's education.

***

Getting Ready for High School

Error #1: Not knowing how (or not being willing) to prepare your child for high school.
Solution: Being prepared is the first step in any successful journey. Today, this especially applies prior to enrolling your child in high school. This preparation will entail talking with your child about five major topics:

1. The purpose of high school;
2. Why high school is the "job" of your child's teenage years;
3. How school and work match up;
4. What school performance records mean; and
5. Dropping out: The range of effects.

***

The Purpose of High School

When talking with your child, first listen to what he or she thinks the purpose of high school is. A simple opening question might be: "Why do teenagers have to go to high school?" You might expect a few of the following responses:

- "To prepare us for a good job."
- "To keep us off the streets and out of trouble."
- "To prepare us for college."
- "To make our parents proud."

After listening to what your child thinks, follow up with the solid knowledge that you have about high school. And on the lighter side, remind your child that if there were no high school, adult life, with all the harder things, would start right after the eighth grade!

Ask your child to think about the purpose of high school in terms of:

- Time and Transitions
- An Opportunity
- Closure

Time and Transitions

High school is about a very special and unique time in our life. It is a once-in-a-lifetime experience. As adults we may attend college as often and as long as we like, but we cannot do the same with high school. It is an environment that is available to us only when we are teenagers.

The high school years are so special that reunions were created so that people could stay connected, reflect on the past, and measure their successes in life after completing the basics.

High school is also about students having to experience several transitions, such as:

- From middle school to high school;
- From a small school population to a larger one;

- From a more restricted to a less restricted school environment (open campuses, for example);
- From childhood to adolescence; and
- From a teenager's perspective to that of a young adult, as students begin to mature in high school.

An Opportunity

High school presents an opportunity. It continues the process begun in elementary and middle school:

- Learning how to interact with others (social skills);
- Practicing being on time to learn (social skills); and
- Learning how to do what is required in order to succeed academically (work skills).

The high school years help students lay the foundation for adult life. They are the teenager's training ground for college and work. High school helps teenagers decide how they want to participate in the game of life as a working member, and what kind of person they want to be. If the opportunity is taken, teenagers can use their high school years to contemplate and plan a future that will allow them to live independent lives.

The opportunity in high school for teenagers is to be able to participate in a system that can help them learn how to think critically and analytically. From this they can be prepared for a wide range of unknown circumstances.

It's important that teenagers have this place to receive information that will allow them to develop their minds and pursue their thoughts and dreams. Receiving information is to a teenager's growth and progress what breathing air is to life. Without air there is no life; without information there is no growth.

Closure

Completing high school can eventually provide a signal of "closure" or completion. It signals to the adult world what teenagers have accomplished as students. The teenagers are now more ready to plunge into the everyday challenges of adult life. They have created a foundation, which can have an effect on their future.

***

High School Is the "Job" of Your Child's Teenage Years

As your discussion continues, ask your child why he thinks high school might be considered his main "job" during his teen years. You'll probably get an interesting response.

- He may not have any idea;
- He may say "It's not!" because he's not getting paid; or
- He may say, "Maybe because we have to go there five days a week. They expect us to do all sorts of work. And if we are late or absent, the teachers are on us!"

Encourage your child to expand on his answers as much as he can. And once again, add your thoughts, considering how your daily work tasks link to what your child will be expected to do.

The next question you should ask is: "Do you want to live with your parents for the rest of your life?" The answer will probably be "No!" If so, ask what your child thinks will be needed to live a successful life apart from you. The most common answer is: "A job, and one that pays well!" What can you add to this response?

Your follow-up question here might be: "What do you need in order to get a well-paying job?" The key answer that you want to draw out is: *"A good education!"*

Give your child three things to focus on in his role as a high school student:

- The Expectations
- The Future
- The Money

The Expectations

Talking about "expectations" at school is very important. A teenager once said to me, "Students should not receive 'D' or 'F' grades, because school is so boring. We should get at least a 'C' grade just for showing up!" I quickly informed the student that it is not reasonable to think that students should get credit for "just" showing up. Setting standards and having expectations of students is a way of measuring if students are learning. Therefore, students must do the work in order to get credit. This means doing one's personal best! Your child's goal as a high school student must be to do his or her personal best.

The Future

In what ways will his future look and feel different if he does or doesn't prepare for it? Help him to understand that learning how to work and to be responsible is a very important job. Explain and emphasize the idea that, as in most things, not planning for the future increases the likelihood of a poor outcome—that is, failure. Succeeding or failing is a "do-it-yourself" job. Your child's planning as a high school student will provide a foundation for the likelihood of his future success!

The Money

Discuss with your child how the economic benefits of successfully completing high school compare with the economic consequences of leaving high school without a diploma.

On average, high school graduates have a greater likelihood of being employed than their dropout counterparts, and the dropouts will earn less money on average when they eventually secure work. For example:

MEDIAN BEGINNING ANNUAL EARNINGS

HIGH SCHOOL GRADUATE	HIGH SCHOOL DROPOUT
$30,732	$22,152

Source: Bureau of Labor Statistics, Current Population Survey, 2009

To make these figures easier to grasp, you can talk in terms of monthly, weekly, daily, and hourly pay:

MEDIAN BEGINNING PAY BY PERIOD

	HIGH SCHOOL GRADUATE ⇩	HIGH SCHOOL DROPOUT ⇩
MONTHLY	$2,561	$1,846
WEEKLY	$591	$426
DAILY	$118	$85
HOURLY	$15	$11

Talk to your child about how he or she can earn money while in high school that can be applied to higher learning. One is the obvious way, by having an extracurricular job. The other is to do an excellent job in the classroom, with the payoff being a scholarship for college! All teenagers like to have money. However, I have met more than a few who either are not doing, or do not know how to do, the work to earn it. Earning money for a job well done, whether inside or outside the classroom, is the sign of someone serious.

***

How School and Work Match Up

It is important to explore with your child the link between the high school life and his or her future as a working person. This is an important discussion to have. Teenagers need to understand that in a large way high school is preparation for functioning later in the work environment. During this key time, parents can help their child move toward success.

The following table illustrates some of the important aspects of the school experience that relate directly to preparing for the work future:

School Life	Work Life
⇩	⇩
Classroom rules, expectations and graduation requirements.	⇨ Workplace rules, expectations and promotion requirements.
Teachers who direct and oversee classroom activities and evaluate outcomes.	⇨ Bosses and supervisors who organize the workplace, set work goals, direct work in progress, and evaluate work completed.
Students are given exams and quizzes to measure performance and progress.	⇨ Employees are given evaluations to measure performance and progress.
Students are given awards, scholarships and recognition for the work they do.	⇨ Employees are given awards, raises and recognition for the work they do.
Students can be expelled from school for breaking minor rules repeatedly, or for one serious infraction.	⇨ Employees can be dismissed from a job for breaking minor rules repeatedly, or for one serious infraction.

***

The Roadblocks

What kinds of things can prevent your child from using his school experience to make a successful transition into his or her work life? Let's take a look:

IN-SCHOOL HABITS	**ON-THE-JOB RESULTS**
⇩	⇩
Constantly late or absent, with or without a reason	⇨ No raise, no promotion, or loss of job!
Can't get along with teachers or fellow students	⇨ No raise, no promotion, or loss of job!
Fails to complete assignments successfully or at least as instructed	⇨ No raise, no promotion, or loss of job!

Remember, high school is the "job" of your child's teenage years. Therefore, you must constantly remind your child that: High school is a four-year job assignment that needs to be completed. *It is preparation for the adult work life!*

On this four-year assignment, learning is the "work" that your teenager is expected to do. Your teenager's job title is "student," and the principal is the boss. The teachers, counselors, and other staff are the supervisors. Your teenager has scheduled days to show up for learning and is expected to arrive on time, and behave in a certain manner.

Your teenager earns credits to show that he is learning. The earned credits will result in a promotion. And, the final successful completion of your teenager's "job" will show that he is prepared for college or adult work life. Some teenagers will do average to above average work, while others will quit (the "dropouts"). But whether your teenager loves it or hates it: *High school is a four-year job assignment that needs to be completed.*

No matter how well, or not so well, your teenager does on this job, he will never experience another quite like it. In addition, no other job will require parents to participate in their child's work by writing a short note when he is late or absent and meet with those in charge to discuss "job performance."

So, once more, whether your teenager loves it or hates it: *High school is a four-year job assignment that needs to be completed.*

***

Teenagers need to know that the habits they develop in school can easily carry over as habits on their job during adulthood. For example, the habit of bad manners and arriving late to work will cost an employer in profits and may cost your child his job. So, emphasize that "Practice makes perfect," for good and for bad! High school students must be mindful of the habits they are forming. No matter what type of work your child chooses to do in life, having positive performance, organizational, and interaction skills is essential!

***

What School Performance Records Mean

It is important to discuss with your child how the high school report card and the transcript are similar to a resume. Begin this conversation by asking your child, "Can you see how your report card and your transcript would be viewed as being similar to a resume?" The answer that you will most likely get is "No."

You must then begin to explain the similarity. As with a resume, the report card and the transcript give a summary of one's work. The report card gives current progress information, and the transcript provides a historic view.

The report card:

- Tells where the student is currently learning (working),
- Gives the description and status of the student's work, and
- Describes the level of the student's performance (grades).

The transcript highlights:

- The student's previously attempted and completed work,
- A pattern of how the student has performed over time, and
- The overall grade point average (overall performance).

Finally, ask your child, "Do you think it is important for an employer hiring a high school student to know how well the student is doing in school?" The answer I generally get from kids is: "No, school has nothing to do with the work they want you to do." Unfortunately, many students do not know that school performance is important to an employer. It is the primary indicator of the child's likelihood of success in the job position. And responsible employers want a balance where neither work nor school performance will suffer due to the other. Explain to your child that you do understand his enthusiasm about working. However, choosing to work should not be at the expense of completing a basic education.

***

Dropping Out:
The Range of Effects

It is important that teenagers understand how the impact of dropping out of school can and will affect not only their own lives, but also the lives of others. Provide your child with a few solid insights as to why completing school is so important. Some of your reasons might encompass the following thoughts:

- When a teenager drops out of school, life will certainly become more difficult—not easier as he or she might envision.
- Dropouts often experience feelings of embarrassment and discomfort during their adult years when asked the very important question while seeking employment: "How many years of education have you completed?"
- One's desirability as a suitable candidate for a job, with prospects for advancement, will drop dramatically. People in hiring positions are rarely pleased or willing to interview teenagers and young adults who have not completed the basics in education. When employers interview a prospective employee, they ask themselves, "What does this applicant have to contribute if he lacks a basic education?"

Often, teenagers feel that they have the capacity to do any job if given the opportunity and training. Eagerness and enthusiasm notwithstanding, they fail to see a couple of stumbling blocks that wouldn't necessarily figure in their thinking:

- The Time Factor
- The Cost Factor

The Time Factor

The Time Factor refers to the very limited amount of time, if any, that an employer would be willing to take to teach an individual the basic skills that should have been learned in school.

The Cost Factor

Right alongside comes the Cost Factor. This goes to the expense of training. How many employers will spend their profit making time to teach fundamentals, when it is just as easy to hire someone who has the required entry skills solidly in place?

- Dropouts are more likely to be unemployed compared to individuals who have higher levels of educational attainment.

- Dropouts are generally perceived as being irresponsible, whether they are or not. When offered employment, they tend to earn less than those with a high school diploma and a post high school education.

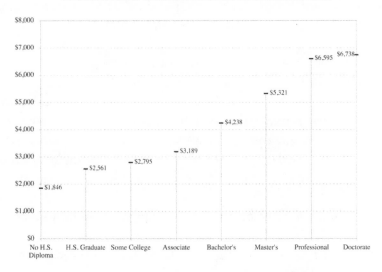

AVERAGE MONTHLY EARNINGS ACCORDING TO EDUCATIONAL LEVEL

Source: Census Bureau, 2009

***

Being in the Best Suited School

Parents enroll their children in a particular school for a variety of reasons:

- Proximity to home;
- Continued familiarity with friends and classmates;
- Siblings or other family members previously attended the school;
- Positive recommendations;

or no particular reason at all.

Error #2: Not enrolling your child in a school that can best meet his or her academic and social needs.

Solution: As a parent you can often exert some influence over the school that your child will attend. The above considerations, and possibly others as well, will most likely figure in. However there is more to think about.

- Get a good idea of what your child dreams or thinks about doing when he is finished with school. Talk to him.

    This is important because in addition to the standard curriculum, various schools may provide specialized course work; and the emphasis on what students are learning will vary. For example, there will be a math emphasis rather than a history or literature emphasis for students taking course work in engineering, and a science emphasis for students taking course work in health. This is well worth your exploration.

- Do some research before choosing a high school for your child.

    Spend a few hours at high schools in which you have an interest. Now, I know that you are probably thinking that you cannot take off work. However, if you live in California, for instance, "The Family—School Partnership Act" allows workers, under clear guidelines, to take off up to 40 hours a school year to conduct school-related business. The law covers employers with 25 or more employees at the same location, and it applies to parents, grandparents and guardians.[1]

Investigate whether similar allowances exist in your area. If they do not, please use whatever free time arrangements are available for making sure that your child's needs are met.

When you make your visits to check out a high school, use your time wisely and efficiently. Arrange beforehand to meet at a set time with an administrator, a counselor, and teachers. Write down any questions you want answered, and bring a pen and pad for taking notes.

There are five (5) questions you should ask school officials on this fact-finding visit, and eight (8) observations you should make. The questions are:

1. What are the overall academic expectations for all students?
2. What are the social interaction guidelines for all students?
3. What is the process in place to ensure that all students are achieving according to the established academic expectations and adhering to the social guidelines?
4. What recourse is used when expectations and guidelines, within and outside of the classroom, are not met?
5. What has been the graduation rate for incoming freshmen over the past four years?

---

1 AB 2590, Ch. 1290, 1994 (Eastin) & AB 47, Ch. 157, 1997 (Murray), CA Labor Code section 230.8

On your visit, if you are able, speak with the campus security officers. They are the most overlooked people on campus. They also can be the eyes and ears of the school. Therefore, they have a lot to share.

Meeting these people will help you get a feel for the school's climate and the culture. This is your right as well as your responsibility. Remember, this is research. Your mission is to find out what will work best for your child!

And the observations are:

1. As you enter the main building, in what ways are you made to feel welcome?

    The manner and degree to which you are made to feel welcome can be an indication that your presence, as well as your child's presence on campus, is appreciated and desired. If you do not see a "Welcome" sign or directions for signing in, please do not hesitate to ask the principal or his/her secretary why these are missing.

2. Are you presented with clear directions stating where visitors must go to sign in?

    Signing in is a comment on school safety. It is important that school officials know who is on campus at any given moment.

3. Once you have reached your sign-in destination, are you treated in a professional, friendly manner, with an offer of assistance?

    This may suggest how you will be treated as a participating parent. It may also say what the educational environment for your child will be apart from the classroom.

    Be aware of the body language of the school personnel; be in tune with their tone, in addition to what they say. These cues will suggest how much or how little your presence is desired. When you are introduced to the person you wish to see, notice whether he or she appreciates that you have taken the time to visit.

4. Does the school have a vision?

Investigate whether the school has a mission statement. This is important. The mission statement says what educators and other adults will do to guide and encourage students to succeed in school and in life. It is also meant to remind students that they are special, that they have a purpose in life. If educators have taken the time to develop a mission statement, they have a vision for the students they are serving.

Several things can occur in a school without vision. It can become a costly yet poorly run baby-sitting service, a dumping ground for uninspired and unmotivated teenagers. It can evolve into a stress-loaded employment site for educators who may or may not be struggling to make a difference in the lives of their students. A school without a vision is a lot like a boat without a rudder. There is a wonderful ancient proverb that reminds us that where there is no vision, people perish.

According to the dictionary the word "perish" means, "(a) To pass from existence, disappear gradually; (b) To spoil or deteriorate."

Many teenagers are disappearing from our public school system. They rarely show up for school; when they do, they only go through the motions of being a student before dropping out. In either case, they are not a part of a very important mission. They are showing no signs of being individuals with a purpose or focus in life. These students have little or no understanding of how education and the work life connect, and as a result they make some poor decisions. Many of them become undesirables and their lives lose purpose.

5. What is the physical condition of the school?

    –   General upkeep of the facility (worn and ragged versus well kept);
    –   Neatness and cleanliness of the administrative areas;
    –   Cleanliness of classrooms, student bathrooms, and cafeteria;
    –   Availability of bathroom supplies for students;
    –   Presence or absence of graffiti;
    –   Visible presence of those charged with plant upkeep (such as custodians, gardeners).

    High school students notice when their school surroundings are dirty, run down, and ill kept. They may wonder: If the adults involved don't care enough to provide for minimum physical needs, how can they have any concern for our educational needs? Unfortunately, when students feel this way, they sometimes decide not to do what is necessary and expected of them.

    The physical appearance of a school should reflect the words of Oscar Wilde:

    "A school should be the most beautiful place in every town and village — so beautiful that the punishment for undutiful children should be that they should be debarred from going to school the following day."

6. Does it appear to be a safe environment?

    Ask to look at the printed procedures to insure student safety. Talk to your variety of hosts about how effectively and consistently they are enforced. Every school should be a safe place for children.

7. How are freshman classes conducted?

    By observing freshman level classes, you will get a feel for what your child will experience on a daily basis.

When you enter a math class, do the learning materials posted on the walls embrace you? Is the teacher's style of teaching exciting to you? Are the students engaged in active learning?

When you enter a science class, do the formulas and experiments displayed in the classroom inspire your curiosity to learn? Can the teacher share his or her knowledge about science in an understandable and captivating way? And again, is the class conducted in a way that encourages student participation?

It is also a good idea to visit several upper level classrooms. Getting a glimpse of what your child will experience as a freshman is good, but getting a glimpse of what is to follow is even better.

8. What is the classroom like under a substitute teacher?

Observe two or more classrooms being taught by a substitute teacher. This is important because you need to know if these teachers can proceed with the ongoing classroom format without disrupting the pace of learning. Are they well versed in the subject(s) they have been assigned to teach? Are they teaching students from a prepared lesson plan?

Bear in mind that if a short-term or long-term substitute teacher who is not proficient in the subject that is assigned to your child's classroom, you need to be concerned about the school's ability to meet your child's learning needs reliably and consistently.

What is your goal with these classroom observations? Perhaps the following passage will help you:

"The attention of children must be lured, caught, and held, like a shy wild animal that must be coaxed with bait to come close. If the situations, the materials, the problems before a child do not interest him, his attention will slip off to what does interest him, and no amount of exhortation or threats will bring it back."

—John Holt

Once you have completed your research, go home and evaluate your visit. Use what works for you. As a suggestion, one way that may help you is to use a format commonly called the "Ben Franklin Method." Make two columns on a piece of paper. Title the first column "Positives" or "+", and title the second column "Negatives" or "-". Then list in the appropriate column how you feel the school met the various items mentioned in our campus visit lookout list. When you have finished this, see which column has the most points listed, and ask yourself:

- Is this the kind of school I want to enroll my child in?
- If I were a teenager, would I benefit from being there?

A simple "yes" or "no" answer will do. Keep in mind that this school will be your child's home away from home, six-plus hours a day, five days a week.

- If your answer is "no", you know that you must continue to research other schools.

- If your answer is "yes", but with a few important reservations, ask yourself these questions:

  - What are my child's chances of succeeding in this environment as it is?
  - Does my child have the temperament to stay focused and do well in the environment?
  - Can I help eliminate the weaknesses at the school I am considering?

Once you have made your choice, consider shadowing your child for a day. It is important that you see your teenager at his learning site. It is equally important that you see your child's teachers in the act of teaching. Keep in mind that you do not have to be a teacher or college-educated to know what good teaching and learning look like.

Use a day to attend classes with your teenager within the first few weeks of school. Observe your teenager at work. After all, attending high school is his or her full-time job.

On a scale of 1 to 10:

- Evaluate how your teenager performs.

  - Was my teenager dressed appropriately for school (work)?
  - Did my teenager arrive at work on time?
  - Did my teenager arrive prepared with the necessary materials that are needed to do a good job (i.e., paper, pen, pencil, books, etc.)?
  - Did my teenager pay attention to the details of his work?
  - Did my teenager have a clear understanding of what was expected of him?
  - Does my teenager have a good work attitude?

- Evaluate the performance of each of your child's teachers.

  - Were the teachers dressed appropriately for work?
  - Did the teachers arrive at class (work) on time?
  - Did the teachers seem prepared to do a good job, ready to teach from a prepared lesson plan?
  - Were the teachers stimulating and encouraging, and did they have a good work attitude?

- Ask each of your child's teachers any questions you may have.

Included might be:

  - What is my child expected to know?
  - What should my child be able to do after completing this course?
  - How is technology (computers, television, and DVDs) used in the classroom and how will it enhance the learning?

***

The Importance of Orientation

Orientation: Introductory instruction concerning a new situation.

Error #3: Failing to attend a school orientation designed for new students and their parents.
Solution: It is important to attend the school's orientation with your child. Here are the reasons:

- To introduce your child to a new school environment;

- To receive written and verbal information that you may not get at a later date, including:

    - School policy and expectations (parent, student & teacher);
    - Promotion and graduation requirements;
    - Curriculum availability and other related information.

- To receive information about special programs and services available to students, including:

    - Tutoring and mentoring programs;
    - School-to-work or career programs;
    - Counseling and other family support services and programs.

- To meet the school's administrative team and other staff members (the counselors, the school's psychologist, etc.). *It is important that you know whether they have moved beyond rhetoric about parental involvement; look for evidence that they actively welcome involved parents.* This will be your opportunity to ask them questions:

    - What are their job duties and responsibilities?
    - What are their views on parent involvement within the school and their definition of this involvement?

- You will have an opportunity to meet other parents and further familiarize yourself with the campus.

What you get out of attending your child's orientation can vary from school to school. So call the school in which you are intending to enroll your child and find out what will be the anticipated benefits of the orientation.

***

Proper Student Registration

Error #4: Failing to follow proper registration guidelines as set out by school officials.
Solution: Follow the registration procedures exactly as detailed. The registration date may even be prior to the first day of instruction. Take advantage of early registration opportunities.

- By registering on the appointed date, your child will have a better chance of being enrolled in classes of his or her choosing (subjects and teachers). Waiting until the first day of school or later may delay the process of getting your child a full schedule of classes. I have personally witnessed students falling behind in credits because they did not register as requested.

- Students are sometimes given perks for registering early. For example, your child could receive a locker and/or a discount on his or her Student ID Card. This can vary from school to school. It would be a good idea to contact the school where you are intending to enroll your child and find out what the perks are!

***

The Participating Parent

Error #5: Being a non-participant in your child's education.

Solution: To insure success at this level, your active participation is a must! There are several roles that you can focus on that will help you along the path toward being an actively participating parent. They are:

- The Fact Finder
- The Record Keeper
- The Coach
- The Accommodator
- The Ally

Being the Fact Finder

What facts should you be gathering, and what basic physical tools does your child need to be a successful high school student? Be keenly aware of what is happening in all aspects of your child's education. Don't be the weak link! Become a "fact finder" by asking lots of questions. Then be proactive on your child's behalf with the facts that you have.

- You must make sure that your teenage son or daughter has the necessary materials to perform well in all classes. This includes books, paper, pens, pencils, highlighters, notebooks, and a calculator—just to name a few. If you cannot provide your teenager with the necessities, look for resources that might be able to help you.

What is the content of your child's classes?

- Get the facts on what your child is expected to learn. Ask every teacher for a copy of the assignment schedule, lesson plan, or syllabus so that you can stay current with what is expected of your child.

What courses, credits, and GPA (Grade Point Average) are required for graduation?

- Speak on a regular basis with a counselor or an administrator to make sure that your teenager is on track to satisfy the requirements in all of these categories. This will help you prevent your child from straying to the point that recovery may seem impossible.

What does it take to advance to the college level, and how can I help?

- There is a difference between the required courses to graduate from high school and those needed to enter a college or a university. You must talk with a counselor or the high school's college advisor to make sure your teenager is on the right track.

In summary, parents who are closely involved with their high school student are aware of:

- What the course work is;
- What the graduation requirements are;
- What their child needs in order to be successful; and
- The difference between courses that are needed to graduate from high school and the courses needed to enter a college or university.

You will never hear these parents say, "I didn't know!"

Being the Record Keeper

"I never travel without my diary."

—Oscar Wilde

Don't let a situation develop in which you are surprised by the lagging progress of your teenager at school. You must stay vigilant and be prepared for any unanticipated problems. Your non-attentiveness will only play into and magnify any difficulties which may have arisen.

This in turn will delay proper completion and graduation day for your teenager.

As a tool to help you stay current with your teenager's scholastic progress, I suggest keeping a "Progress Log." It can contain information of the following type:

- The Academic Program (Class Schedule)

    - What courses your child is taking;
    - At what times and in what classrooms do they meet?
    - The names of the teachers;

This information is important because it lets you know:

    - Your teenager's academic direction;
    - Expected whereabouts on campus; and
    - A contact for your academic concerns.

- Status Changes

    Keep track of your child's class changes (adds/drops), and any grade changes. Any of these modifications can affect:

    - Your child's GPA (Grade Point Average);
    - Academic promotion to the next grade level;
    - Timely fulfillment of course work required for academic completion; and
    - On-time graduation.

- Progress Documentation

    - A copy of all of your teenager's report cards;
    - The most current copy of your child's transcript; and
    - Transcripts from other schools where additional classes were taken.

- A Copy of Attendance Records

This information is important because it helps you:

- Monitor your teenager's attendance;
- See how absences will affect your child's grades; and
- Understand how unexplained absences may indicate that other more serious problems are in play.

- Allocated Required Materials

  - A list of books and equipment

It is important to know that the school has provided your child with those materials, which are standard for at least minimal class participation. Also, all books and equipment must be returned at the end of each school year. If any of these items have been lost or stolen, there may be monetary or other penalties.

- Meeting Notes

Take notes when meeting with your child's teachers and other school officials. Keep these notes. It is important to have a good recollection of the details of these conversations regarding your child. With so many things going on in your life, this will help you to recall easily.

Being the Coach

"No man is an island."

—John Donne

Children cannot be ignored and left alone to accomplish great things. Be a coach to your child. I have lost count of the number of students who are not experiencing a learning connection. These students do not know what is going on in their classes on several levels. Perhaps an advocate, a coach, is what is lacking.

I have met and worked with many parents. Those who performed the role of a coach clearly understood that the four years prior to a young person officially becoming an adult are just as important as the first four years of one's life. As your child's coach, much like the coach of any team, you are in the position to take a broad view of how his education is progressing.

- *You are coaching your child to become a Most Valuable Student (MVS), because there are colleges and businesses that are looking for the most talented and the brightest high school graduates. You must work with your child to stay on course.*

- If your child is not succeeding at his job of learning, it becomes your role as coach to dialogue with others to:

  - Discover what is hindering your child's success;
  - Develop and evaluate what steps can be taken to improve performance; and
  - Decide who will be responsible for implementing various pieces of the revised success strategies.

Here are a few ideas on what success strategies you should take into consideration:

- Helping your child value the importance of preparation and receptivity for learning.

  Learning can only occur under the right circumstances. It has been said, and is certainly true, that "When the student is ready, the teacher will appear." Help your child make the teacher appear!

- Helping your child find his identity as a student.

If your child can draw a sense of unique purpose and importance from being a successful student, this will help you develop the guiding steps and support that are needed.

Samuel Butler said it best: "Every man's work, whether it be literature or music or pictures or architecture or anything else, is always a portrait of himself."

You can view your child's education as a self-competition, but it is one that he must win. Your achievement goal for your child is that he or she will gain admission to one or more of the best colleges in the country. You are coaching your child to become a Most Valuable Student (MVS)!

Therefore:

- Make sure your child studies.

    – This is practicing the skill of learning

- Monitor homework assignments, review them, and talk to your teenager about them.

    Homework is important. It helps students reflect on and evaluate the information presented during the day. Homework is also how students prepare for tests. Don't hesitate to request that your teenager be given homework assignments. But in doing so, you must assure the teachers that the assignments will be completed and turned in on time. As your child's coach, you will be helping him or her develop into their personal best.

- Get feedback in regard to your child's performance.

    Your feedback will come from carefully reading your child's report card. The report card is your evidence of performance. It contains important information regarding your child's progress. There are obvious indicators on a report card (the teacher's comments) that suggest why parents might contact their child's teacher(s). The following are a few examples:

- Student is in danger of failing;
- Student needs to complete assignments;
- Student needs to improve attitude.

You can obtain illuminating information from your conversations with your child's teachers and other school officials.

- While coaching your child, you must ask lots of questions.

  Get a deeper understanding of what your child sees as expectations of himself as a high school student. This can be your most challenging task, but most certainly worth pursuing. Unfortunately, many parents ask, "How" was school today?" And, of course the answer is usually "Fine" or "OK". Instead, by asking your teenager "what" he or she has learned in school, you can better determine how well your child paid attention and is understanding, what is being taught in class.

  Start by asking your child what he learned in his first period class. Then ask about the second period class, third period class, etc. Keep in mind if you ask your child what he learned in school today, and the answer is "Nothing," you'd better dig deeper!

Being the Accommodator

It is important to be helpful to teachers, administrators, and other school officials. Provide them with information that will help them do their jobs effectively and efficiently for your child. Be accessible to teachers. Make it easy for them to get in touch with you. It is important to meet routinely with teachers and other educators to discover what you can do together to assist in your child's success.

- Build a Bridge between Your Home and the School.

Give school officials information that can build the bridge between your home and the school. Assure them that you can be contacted in any medical, social, or academic emergency involving your child.

Provide school officials with:

- Your current telephone number and home address;
- Your work telephone number;
- Information about a contact person if you can't be reached in an emergency; and
- Information concerning your child's health.

- Make Periodic Phone Calls and Visits to Your Teenager's Teachers.

It is important to understand the workload of teachers:

- Preparing a daily lesson plan for one or more subjects;
- Teaching several classes a day;
- Grading exams and homework assignments;
- Maintaining classroom discipline;
- And, for many teachers, parenting their own children.

High school teachers do not have the luxury of telephoning or sending all parents a short note as an update on their teenagers' progress. Home visits are rarities.

Many parents I have met have security alarms on their cars and in their homes, to which they would never give access to a stranger. How odd it seems to give our children over to complete strangers for six or more hours a day, five days a week.

It is up to you to be proactive in keeping the lines of communication open. Contact and meet regularly with the people who have a direct influence on your child. Be supportive and consistent in following through on the recommendations of your child's teachers.

After all, it is the teacher's job to provide a service that will best serve your child's educational needs.

- Be a Contributor!

Do what you can to make things better. You live in your community. Be willing to invest in raising the level of your child's educational experience. There are many things you can give: time, money, books equipment, etc. Give in any way that you can!

Being the Ally

For the sake of your child, you must strive to be an ally to teachers and other educators. When cooperation between parents and teachers exists, our children have a greater likelihood of success. Often, our teenagers see or imagine that parents and teachers are in conflict. Teenagers need their parents and teachers to be allies. This alliance can yield major results.

- Initiate the parent / teacher relationship.

Take the first step in making sure your child sees the parent and teacher as partners rather than adversaries. After all, you are delivering your child to individuals who will teach as well as influence your child. Working together, parents and teachers can have a significant impact on school life. When parents and educators align, they present a most formidable team. Students can witness the strength that this unity creates. They will feel it moving them toward greater heights. The school environment will be positively affected, resulting in attitude changes and performance improvements from the students.

- Put positive role modeling into action.

Parents and educators are role models for our children. James Baldwin said, "Children have never been good at listening to their elders, but they have never failed to imitate them." And Matthew Arnold tells us, "Conduct is three-fourths of our life and its largest concern." If these statements are true we cannot overrate how our young people view the parent/teacher interactions.

Students get the modeling that is needed to function as adults from the two most powerful sets of people in their lives: their parents and their teachers. If children see their parents interacting positively with teachers, it will influence how the children, in turn, will act toward their teachers.

- Support teachers for not tolerating unacceptable school place behavior.

It is the teacher's job to teach, not to manage ongoing rudeness and disrespect from, or between, the students. Tell your child that while it is acceptable to dislike the personality and the attitude of others, at the same time you will not tolerate any outburst of disrespectful behavior at school. If your child does behave disrespectfully toward his or her teachers, make quick contact to offer your support for the school-sanctioned disciplines, and to offer an apology.

***

Covering the Bases

Error #6: Not asking for the help of others when you can't fully and actively participate in your child's education.
Solution: Delegate important responsibilities to a trusted friend or relative if you cannot fulfill important parental responsibilities.

Delegating is a most critical and extremely important step for a successful journey on the path of doing.

When your teenager is doing poorly in school and you aren't actively involved, your inaction will be viewed as neglect. Enlisting the help of others sends a powerful message to your teenager's teachers. It says that you are a caring and attentive parent who is not willing to watch your teenager fail. It also tells your teenager:

- I care about you, and
- I will do whatever I can to help you succeed in school.

***

Stopping the Slide

Error #7: Failing to take immediate action when first hearing that your child may be on the road to failure.

Solution: Within the first grading periods, if signs appear that your teenager is not succeeding in school, heed this serious warning!

You must take a proactive approach to correct this straying off course. This is a critical opportunity that is often missed. I have seen too many students fail to graduate from high school because timely action was not taken by the parents when the trouble signs began to arise. Here are some of the indicators that prompt action is required.

- Credits not being earned in an anticipated steady fashion;
- Ongoing complaints that classroom failings are because the teachers can't teach;
- A continuing pattern of lateness and absences;
- Repetitive behavioral disciplines or suspensions;
- An administratively imposed restriction on the amount of time your child is allowed to attend school daily.

Here's what you can do:

- As was previously mentioned in the section <u>Being the Ally</u>, you can work more closely with your teenager and his teachers, regardless of how challenging this may be for you.

- Consider enrolling your teenager in another school. It does not make sense to have your child situated where his various needs are not being addressed. Perhaps your child's needs will be better served:

- In a more intimate school setting;
- On a closed campus (where students are not allowed to leave campus during the course of the school day);
- In a more structured environment;
- Or by adjusting other factors that concern you about your child's current school situation.

***

Chapter Three

The Path of Knowing: Moving Deeper into the Journey

"Knowledge is power"

—Francis Bacon

This part of the journey concerns knowing your duties and responsibilities as a partner in your child's education. Communicating with your child's teachers and understanding how teachers want your participation is vitally important. In this chapter, five (5) sections will ask you to place your focus on the following ideas:

- Education Is a Fitness Program.
- You Have Commonality with the Teachers.
- The Parent/Teacher Relationship Is Special.
- Your Visible Participation Is Vital.
- Reinforcing "School Rules" with Your Teenager Is Critical.

***

Education Is a Fitness Program

As a parent you want your child to be intellectually fit for his or her life as an adult. You want your child to have a good job, good health, and happiness. Education is an academic and social fitness program, and it starts in the home. It is a program that teaches children social skills, as well as subject matter that will prepare them for life.

You are your child's first teacher. Educators will expect that you have worked with your child on social skills. The teachers will work, along with you, to help your child with academic and vocational learning. High school teachers are relying on you to send them teenagers who are well behaved, willing, and prepared to learn.

***

You Have Commonality with Teachers

Pay attention to what commonalties you share with your child's teachers. These similarities bind parents and teachers working together toward a student's benefit. Therefore, pay attention to what you have in common! It is easier to communicate effectively if you identify the following shared points:

- Common Expectations

  As a parent, based on your efforts in raising your children, you hope and expect that they will surpass you as societal contributors. Teachers harbor similar expectations for their students in the arena of learning. And you both attempt to accomplish this in nurturing and caring ways.

- Common Responsibility

  Both parents and teachers must model behavior from which children can learn and grow. As parents you must model behavior that introduces your children to what it means to be human and how to behave. Teachers must model workplace behavior when in the presence of your children.

  Parents and teachers both experience the praise and pride when children do well. But parents and educators also often endure the pain of blame: parents for children's shortcomings and failures, and teachers for the students who did not learn.

- Common Purpose

  Good parents are very serious about the job of parenting; good educators are very serious about the job of teaching. It takes a special kind of person to both raise children and also work with other's children. Parents and teachers must be mentally and spiritually strong. They must not only love and like children, but also have patience with them.

- Common Status as Elders

  You may balk at the term "elder," but you are older and more mature, and you carry a lifetime of experience to offer in regard to making decisions. You supply our children's largest and most critical support system. When elders unite for the purpose of helping children succeed in school and in life, everyone benefits. When elders choose not to work as a team, our children begin to fall through the cracks of life. This simply means that our children's hearts, minds, and souls are not being touched in a way that leads them into meaningful and productive lives.

As one of many elders, you must never forget:

You are	*E* nlightened	⇨	Time and experiences have helped you develop a better understanding about life.
You have	*L* ongevity	⇨	You have a track record of life's experiences.
You are	*D* ecisive	⇨	You have experience in making difficult decisions.
You are	*E* ducators	⇨	You are healers and leaders.
You are	*R* esilient	⇨	You have stamina, and are hopeful about life.
You are	*S* pecial	⇨	You have a legacy to share, and a special kind of love and respect for life that happens through the process of aging.

***

The Parent/Teacher Relationship Is Special

The educational process works best for your child when you are able to recognize the specialness of the parent/teacher relationship. It is important to pay attention to this relationship. Understanding it will help you to communicate more effectively with your teenager's teachers. By its very nature, it usually is:

- Limited by Time and Place

Your child will have many teachers over four years. Develop a relationship with each of them. You must find the time to meet and talk with the people who will spend a brief, yet very influential, amount of time with your child.

- Built Primarily on Trust and Faith

As a parent you trust educators to help your teenager make a successful transition from school life to college and/or work life. Educators are trusting you to send them teenagers who are well behaved and willing to learn. And you both have faith that the other will do his part!

The high school years are transitional. Parents and educators must work together to guide and introduce teenagers to a new world. The first year can be especially difficult. Students are going through a period of adjustment to a new environment and to different rules. For many it is like visiting a foreign country: the language and the customs are unfamiliar. Learning for these students becomes very difficult when they are not prepared for this new environment. Therefore, parents must model the kind of behavior that will inspire teenagers to learn the language and customs within the school. Educators need parents to help students see the value of what they are learning.

Preparing teenagers for adulthood is not an easy task, and educators need you to assist them. Educators need your assistance because their expertise lies in the teaching of academics and vocational skills. Very few educators are able to teach students who lack discipline, are not interested in learning, or cannot see the connection between education and the work life. Being disciplined and able to see how to make connections is a much-needed skill.

***

Your Visible Participation Is Vital

Education works best for our youth when parents are a visible force in their child's education. Be aware of this most important function and responsibility while on The Path of Knowing. The students of parents who are visible are treated differently than students whose parents are not. *Be visible! There is power in your presence.*

Periodic visits to your teenager's high school make powerful statements to the teachers, the administrators, and your teenager. Statements that say:

- You Have High Expectations

  - These are of your teenager, his teachers, and the administrators. You are willing to work with all three to see that your expectations are met.

- You Are Aware

  - You know about your teenager's work habits and activities at school.
  - Also, you know when and what time is needed to contribute to meeting with your teenager's teachers.

- You Are the Parent That Educators Welcome

  - You will make whatever contributions needed, and allow no excuses, while keeping your teenager on the track of success!

Please be aware that being visible, especially if your child is doing poorly in school, will make a difference in how your child is treated by educators. Not being there to support and coach your child to be a good student will lessen his chances of succeeding in school.

***

Reinforcing "School Rules" with Your Teenager Is Critical

When parents insist that their teenager follow rules set forward within the school environment, the path to outstanding educational results can be greatly facilitated. When you support teachers regarding guidelines and discipline, learning for your child—and teaching—becomes easier. It becomes easier to work together with your child's teachers when you support them in this area.

Many high school students are quick to tell educators that only their parents have the right to tell them what to do. But educators create rules to establish a structure for attaining standards and maintaining a safe environment for everyone. It is critical that you support your teenager's adherence to the rules; they are designed to help everyone reach shared educational goals.

***

The Rules for Success

In my work, I have observed that there are a number of widely held rules which foster academic and social success at school. When students follow these rules there are benefits to be gained; when they do not follow these rules there are short-term and long-term consequences. Here they are, along with some thoughts on why you need to be mindful of them:

Five Rules for Academic Success

- The Attendance Rule
- The Preparation Rule
- The Participating and Completing Assignments Rule
- The Connection Rule
- The Tutoring Rule

The Attendance Rule

- When students choose to not show up, no classroom learning occurs. Your child must show up in order to learn! Students who do not attend all of their classes daily are delaying graduation day.

- Students must arrive at all classes on time. Teachers have limited time to take the roll, collect homework assignments, implement the daily lesson plan, and assign homework. When students are late they are being rude and disrespectful of the teacher's, and their classmates', time. They are also missing out on information that can make a difference in the grade they will earn.

The Preparation Rule

"Man is a tool-using animal. Without tools he is nothing, with tools he is all."

—Thomas Carlyle

- Students must take their tools to class!

  Your child must come to school prepared to learn. This means bringing required materials (tools) to class (including books, paper, pen, pencil, dictionary etc.). I also recommend that students have a daily planner to:

  – Record homework assignments and test dates; and
  – Keep records of all graded tests and assignments. *This is important.* It minimizes surprises, and grading errors can be corrected immediately.

Many wonderful things can and will happen to students who arrive in class with their much-needed tools. For example:

- Learning becomes easier.
- It can be fun.
- Opportunities become available to students who are prepared.

Conversely, when teenagers choose not to bring needed materials to class, it sends a powerful message to teachers that says, "I am not serious about learning."

The Participation and Completing Assignments Rule

Your child must participate in class and complete assignments. Students are required to complete and submit all assignments. What is the point of doing assignments if they are not turned in? Not taking care of both parts of this Rule will obviously affect a student's grades.

Participating in class helps students learn how to do two things:

- Stay focused and on task; and
- Present themselves to a group.

The Connection Rule

- Strongly encourage your teenager to get the telephone numbers of, and stay connected with, at least two other students who are attending and achieving in each of his or her classes. Reasons to do this are:

    - In case of absence, your teenager can find out what occurred in class;
    - He has a way to get assignments for timely submission.

It is important not to get behind in assignments. It is much harder to play catch-up, and there is nothing worse than returning to school and feeling lost. The <u>Connection Rule</u> provides a good way to make friends with people who are on task.

The Tutoring Rule

Everyone needs a coach at some time, in some area of life. Tutoring is about receiving coaching in a particular subject(s). Mistakenly, many students believe that those who do well in school are either born smart or are just lucky. This is not true. Students who are doing well in school are not ashamed of getting help; and they STUDY.

Two Rules for Social Success

- The Respect Rule
- The Good Association Rule

Again, when students follow rules there are benefits to be gained—and there are consequences when rules are not followed!

The Respect Rule

- There are benefits to be gained by respecting others. Your child must show respect toward his teachers and other elders. Both play an important role in our society, and our children need their support and wisdom. Teachers and elders are a good resource for students when they are seeking employment and trying to get into colleges. If students want to be spoken highly of, and offered opportunities, they must treat their elders in a respectful manner.

- School property should not be defaced and destroyed. This includes abusing furniture and equipment, writing graffiti, breaking windows, starting fires, and other like activities. Respect for school property is more than having good manners. When students do these kinds of things they are disrespecting the rights of others to function in a neat, clean, and safe environment. They also affect how public education money is spent. For instance, money that would probably be allotted to purchasing students' books and supplies must be spent on damage repair and replacement.

- Students who choose to use profanity at school in the presence of teachers and other adults are disrespecting a group of people they rely on. This again, though, is about more than having good manners. Profanity in the school arena disrupts civility, is offensive, and is viewed as contributing to acts of violence.

The Good Association Rule

- Everyone needs friends. However, I cannot overstate the importance of your child choosing his friends carefully. It is critical that your teenager recognize that the majority of the students in school are not having a problem getting along with their schoolmates and classmates. It is important that your child make friends with people who are in school and focusing on creating a future of which they can be proud.

- Teenagers who are not attending school and are asking your child to hang with them during school time are not your child's best choices. A true friend would not distract one from getting an education.

- There are more than enough students to observe and copy; most students are getting along with one another.

"Tis better to be alone, than in bad company."

—George Washington

Chapter Four

Completing the Journey:
The Path of Interventions

Aristotle was once asked, *"What is the difference between an educated and an uneducated man?"* He replied, *"The same difference as between being alive and being dead."* With this in mind, you know that you must continue the journey.

Outlasting Fatigue and Frustration

If you have done your best, but your best is not working—seek help. You know that you must not leave your child's future to chance if he is not succeeding in high school. Move beyond any emotions of pain or or frustrations, even if you are feeling that you do not have the strength or the energy to do so. You must continue this journey. You must enter the Path of Interventions because:

- You want your child to have a basic education (the K through 12 program).
- No one cares for your child as deeply as you do.

You must not give up on your child. You must not allow your heartaches and disappointments to get in the way of the goal.

The Path of Interventions involves reaching out to others for help—for your child and for yourself.

***

Getting Help for Your Child

Getting help for your child may be easier than you think. You will need to seek additional assistance and support. It means reaching out to people who are aware of resources and programs that will help your child. What kind of intervention(s) you try will depend on the extent of your child's difficulties, and on the stage at which they surface along the academic pathway.

The following are various kinds of interventions that you might consider:

- Family Involvement

    Your child may simply need you and other family members to spend more time focused on schoolwork with him or her.

- An Academic Coach

There may be those who work either on campus, or apart from the school's setting, providing tutoring (academic coaches). Some students may do better when they receive help from a college student or a volunteer from the community.

- A Mentor

Your child may need a special friend or advisor who will guide him to do his personal best. It could be someone close to his age or a little older. It could be someone he admires and respects.

- Counseling

Your child may need to talk with a professional counselor or therapist. This would be someone with whom he can speak, and resolve problems, in confidence.

- Another School

Your child may be in a school that is unable to meet his or her needs. Persistent difficulties could be a sign that it is time to think about a transfer into another school. Find out what other schools are an option for your child, both within and beyond your district. Other school or program options include:

- An Alternative High School

An Alternative High School is generally a smaller environment. It is for teenagers who are having a hard time adjusting in a regular high school environment. Check with school officials for the procedures to enroll in an Alternative High School. The criterion and procedure can vary within school districts. For example, students may need to be tested or interviewed before enrolling.

- Continuation School

  A Continuation School is also generally a smaller environment. It is for teens that need to be removed from their regular high school setting. It gives students who are deficient in credits the opportunity to complete the high school graduation plan. It is for the hard-to-reach students who are viewed as being a disciplinary problem. Attendance is compulsory.

- Independent Study

  This program is for the student who prefers to work independently. It is an alternative to classroom instruction. Check with school officials for the details of what is expected of students and how the program works within your school district.

OTHER COMPLETION ALTERNATIVES

Finally, if your child is 17 or older, with a grade level status of sophomore or lower after three years of high school, other educational alternatives for completion must be sought. If standard high school is just not working out, it may be important that your child depart—but only after other resources are in place and available. It may mean completing a basic education, with dignity, in a non-traditional educational program. Ask school officials what alternate options are available to help your child be recognized as having completed his education. These options may include:

The High School Proficiency Exam

- In California, the CHSPE (California High School Proficiency Examination) is a pass no pass test. Your child may leave school if he is 16 or older, or has completed the tenth grade and has verified parental permission to leave high school. There is a fee. Check with your State Department of Education for this type of exam.

The GED Program

- The GED (General Educational Development) Program will allow your child the opportunity to earn an equivalency diploma. This diploma will enhance your child's chances of finding a job. The age at which your child can enroll in a GED program varies from state to state.

Job Corps

- Job Corps offers a variety of training programs. Your child can earn his high school diploma or high school equivalency (GED). Your child will learn at his own pace. Job Corps offers this opportunity to individuals who are 16 through 24 years of age.

A Local Education and Employment Training Program

- This type of program varies from state to state. It can offer basic education related to job training or GED preparation and job training.

Adult School

- Adult school is for people 18 and older. However, check with the Department of Education within your state to find out at what age a student can receive an exemption from high school to enroll in adult school. Your child can receive a high school diploma or a GED.

Look into these alternatives with one very important question in mind:

- What is the completion success rate of individuals enrolled?

***

What If...?

If your child is adamant about not completing high school, do the following.

- Write your child a letter and make sure you send this letter through the U.S. Postal Service, Priority Mail.
- Avoid emailing, text messaging or twittering this important and heartfelt message. This is not the same as communicating a message of high importance wrapped in an envelope that says: "PRIORITY".

In this letter, bring to your child's attention:

- How much you appreciate the things that he does well and how proud you are of him;
- How happy you are that he is your child and what you want for him;
- What you understand about his difficulty to experience high school success;
- Your role and responsibility as a parent to support him on this journey to complete a basic education before he becomes an adult; and
- End your letter by talking about your life as a teenager in high school.

This is *your story*. It is critical that your child can get a sense of your young life and see what is similar and different in his life. The following are examples of what you might want to include:

- The type of student you were; be honest. Talk about your attendance, grades, attitude and behavior;
- What you liked and disliked about school;
- What it felt like to graduate or not graduate from high school; and
- How you have benefited in life by graduating from high school.

One more thing, have your friends and family members send your child a letter. They can share their heartfelt concerns about your child's unbending desire to drop out of school, and tell their story. Again, make sure these letters are also sent through the U.S. Postal Service, Priority Mail. Hopefully, your letter and letters from friends and family members will encourage your child to remain in school.

If your child is still adamant about not completing high school, discuss the pros and cons of this decision. Also, have your child do three (3) things:

1. Speak to, or write a short letter to, several people who dropped out of school, to check out how they managed to do well—or not so well—in life after dropping out. This will at least help your child develop a real picture as to whether this is a road he or she wants to take.

2. Know actually what he will be "dropping into," when making the decision to drop out of school. It is pointless to drop out with nowhere to go.

3. Be respectful of others if he chooses to drop out of high school. In other words, do not become a financial burden to family members, friends, or the taxpayers. It is important that your child not make life difficult for others in order to provide for himself or herself.

***

Getting Help for Yourself

In order to help your child succeed, you may need help. You will need the support and encouragement of other people, and you must start the conversation! Talking to other people will help you release feelings of embarrassment and disappointment about your child's lack of success as a high school student. *It is important that you reach out to people who are skilled at helping parents having difficulties with their child, whether the problems relate to school or to upbringing.* Here are some suggestions:

Family Members

- Sometimes your greatest support can come from family. Don't underestimate their concern and potential wisdom!

Spiritual Community

- If you are in fellowship with a particular spiritual community, gather help, support, and information from leaders and other members. Approaching difficult situations from this perspective can often be very helpful.

School Officials

- Ask an administrator, counselor, or staff person if support programs or services exist for parents of failing students. Someone at your child's school should be aware of parenting workshops and support groups.

- Talk with the superintendent of schools, especially if you feel your child is the victim of ineffective classroom instruction or suspect curriculum.

Agencies

- Make an appointment to speak with a licensed family therapist or counselor. Be assured that they are professionally guided by rules of confidentiality.

- Scout out the telephone directory. There should be a number of listings to guide you to family support services.

- Contact the nearest Department of Social Services for help.

Since your personal troubles will always have an impact on your child, you may also want to consider individual counseling if you need help for:

- Stress reduction
- Relationship problems
- Employment problems
- Anger management
- Alcoholism or other addictions
- Child or spousal abuse (as victim or perpetrator)

***

Epilogue

As I stated earlier, never give up. If you give up, who will be there for your child? Reach out as far as you can to help your child. Reach out to as many people as you can. Reach out to those in the political arena if you feel it is necessary: the mayor of your city, the governor of your state. After all, these people had education agendas, which they promoted as reasons to vote for them.

Getting through high school is an important portion of your child's life. Yet having a sense of direction will help you realize that this experience, as difficult as it may sometimes become, is manageable and temporary. Your feelings of sadness, frustration and disappointment, otherwise known here as "the Blues," will pass. Fresh difficult situations will come and go as well. What is lasting is what will result when you put to work what you have read here. You will have helped your child design his future as a productive, successful individual.

Workbook

Your Commitments and Reflections Will Help Guide You!

***

To-Do List

"Imagination is more important than knowledge."
—Einstein

Your To-Do List helps your imagination in assisting to make your teenager's journey successful. It is a record of what you think you need to do and when you need to do it.

If you are about to enroll your teenager in high school, use this section to think about what you can do to give your child a solid start. Visualize what you need to do and do it! Wishing and hoping that your child will be a successful student is not good enough. It is what you are willing to do. Develop a strategy and specific goals to help your child succeed.

If your teenager is currently enrolled in high school and is traveling on a road that is leading to dropping out due to:

- A poor attitude toward school,
- Poor attendance at school, or
- Academic underachievement,

you must take charge of your teenager's high school education. *Take Back the Wheel* and make your teenager's high school journey successful. You must decide what you will do to get your child on the right track. This also means finding a way to establish positive interactions with the teachers and other school officials. So use your imagination to make things right: write it down and then do it!

Use the following pages to document your commitments. Also, do not forget to write on your To-Do List when and what you will do to celebrate your child's achievements and show teachers your appreciation.

***

JOURNAL

Your Journal contains your reflections about what is happening and how you are feeling about your child's education at the high school level. Writing in a journal helps you think more deeply about your role in your child's education and how you can be effective. View your journal as an opportunity to have a conversation with yourself, to ask yourself questions and to answer those questions.

Begin writing in your journal the moment your teenager enters high school. If your child has been in high school for more than a year, just start recording. Record your overall observations about your child's education, your thoughts and your feelings about what you desire for your child, etc.

Also, use your journal to write down what you might want to say to your child's teachers and other school officials; and practice saying the words, especially if you are shy or uncomfortable when talking with educators.

Use the following pages to make your monthly recordings. You may find that you want to write more than once a month, and that is OK. What is important is that you use this section to express yourself.

A final suggestion, use these pages of the book to record scheduled appointments with school officials and too take notes.

***

The following are examples of monthly: To-Do List entries.

- ✓ Attend orientation for new students and parents.

- ✓ Take advantage of early registration opportunities.

- ✓ Get the necessary supplies that will help my teenager succeed in school.

- ✓ Ask my teenager daily: how was your work (school) day?

- ✓ Spend a day on campus meeting teachers.

- ✓ Get a copy of my teenager's class schedule. It is critical that I know what academic program my child is in.

- ✓ Get a copy of the school's calendar of events. It is important that I know the dates of each grading period and semester.

- ✓ Ask my teenager: what did you learn today in each of your classes? If the answer is: nothing, in one or more classes, I need to find out why!

- ✓ Discuss with my teenager, how the level of his education will have an impact on his future.

- ✓ Get a copy of my teenager's report card.

- ✓ Take immediate action! My teenager's report card was not good.

- ✓ Get my teenager an academic coach (tutor).

- ✓ Check in with teachers to see how my teenager is doing in school.

- ✓ Take immediate action! My teenager's behavior at school is unacceptable.

- ✓ Attend parent/teacher meeting.

- ✓ Make plans to celebrate! My teenager's report card was good.

- ✓ Tell my teenager that I am proud of him and how much I appreciate the good work he is doing in school.

- ✓ Get a copy of my teenager's transcript.

- ✓ Take immediate action! My teenager has not been attending school.

- ✓ Attend parent support group meeting.

- ✓ Take immediate action! My teenager will not be promoted to the next grade level.

- ✓ Get my teenager a mentor.

✓ Make plans to celebrate! My teenager will be promoted to the next grade level.

✓ Take immediate action! My teenager will not be graduating.

✓ Meet with the counselor to discuss what other schools or programs are an option for my teenager.

✓ Make plans to celebrate! My teenager will be graduating from high school!

✓ Send each of my teenager's teachers a short note or card expressing my appreciation for their hard work.

So, there you have it. A few examples of the kinds of things you might want to put on your monthly "To-Do List" as your teenager makes his or her journey through high school.

One more thing, as I stated at the beginning of the book: Behind every successful student is an involved parent. Your child will be spending four-years in high school. So, do your best to help your child enter adulthood as a high school graduate. Your child and his teachers are counting on you!

My Teenager's First Year in High School

To-Do List

August

_____

_____

_____

_____

_____

_____

_____

_____

_____

_____

_____

Journal

August

_____

_____

_____

_____

_____

_____

_____

_____

_____

_____

_____

To-Do List
September

_____

_____

_____

_____

_____

_____

_____

_____

_____

_____

Journal
September

_____

_____

_____

_____

_____

_____

_____

_____

_____

_____

_____

To-Do List
October

_____

_____

_____

_____

_____

_____

_____

_____

_____

_____

_____

Journal
October

_____

_____

_____

_____

_____

_____

_____

_____

_____

_____

_____

To-Do List
November

_____

_____

_____

_____

_____

_____

_____

_____

_____

_____

Journal
November

_____

_____

_____

_____

_____

_____

_____

_____

_____

_____

_____

To-Do List
December

_____

_____

_____

_____

_____

_____

_____

_____

_____

_____

_____

_____

Journal
December

_____

_____

_____

_____

_____

_____

_____

_____

_____

_____

_____

_____

To-Do List
January

_____

_____

_____

_____

_____

_____

_____

_____

_____

_____

Journal
January

_____

_____

_____

_____

_____

_____

_____

_____

_____

_____

To-Do List
February

_____

_____

_____

_____

_____

_____

_____

_____

_____

_____

_____

Journal
February

_____

_____

_____

_____

_____

_____

_____

_____

_____

_____

_____

To-Do List
March

_____
_____
_____
_____
_____
_____
_____
_____
_____
_____

Journal
March

_____
_____
_____
_____
_____
_____
_____
_____
_____
_____

To-Do List
April

_____

_____

_____

_____

_____

_____

_____

_____

_____

_____

_____

Journal
April

_____

_____

_____

_____

_____

_____

_____

_____

_____

_____

_____

_____

To-Do List
May

_____

_____

_____

_____

_____

_____

_____

_____

_____

_____

_____

_____

Journal
May

_____

_____

_____

_____

_____

_____

_____

_____

_____

_____

_____

_____

_____

To-Do List
June

_____

_____

_____

_____

_____

_____

_____

_____

_____

_____

_____

_____

Journal
June

_____

_____

_____

_____

_____

_____

_____

_____

_____

_____

_____

_____

To-Do List
July

_____

_____

_____

_____

_____

_____

_____

_____

_____

_____

_____

Journal
July

_____

_____

_____

_____

_____

_____

_____

_____

_____

_____

_____

My Teenager's Second Year in High School

To-Do List

August

_____
_____
_____
_____
_____
_____
_____
_____
_____
_____

Journal

August

_____
_____
_____
_____
_____
_____
_____
_____
_____
_____

To-Do List
September

_____

_____

_____

_____

_____

_____

_____

_____

_____

_____

Journal
September

_____

_____

_____

_____

_____

_____

_____

_____

_____

_____

To-Do List
October

_____

_____

_____

_____

_____

_____

_____

_____

_____

_____

_____

_____

Journal
October

_____

_____

_____

_____

_____

_____

_____

_____

_____

_____

_____

_____

To-Do List
November

_____
_____
_____
_____
_____
_____
_____
_____
_____
_____
_____

Journal
November

_____
_____
_____
_____
_____
_____
_____
_____
_____
_____
_____

To-Do List
December

_____
_____
_____
_____
_____
_____
_____
_____
_____
_____
_____
_____

Journal
December

_____
_____
_____
_____
_____
_____
_____
_____
_____
_____
_____
_____

To-Do List
January

_____
_____
_____
_____
_____
_____
_____
_____
_____
_____
_____

Journal
January

_____
_____
_____
_____
_____
_____
_____
_____
_____
_____
_____

To-Do List
February

_____

_____

_____

_____

_____

_____

_____

_____

_____

_____

Journal
February

_____

_____

_____

_____

_____

_____

_____

_____

_____

_____

To-Do List
March

_____
_____
_____
_____
_____
_____
_____
_____
_____
_____
_____

Journal
March

_____
_____
_____
_____
_____
_____
_____
_____
_____
_____
_____

To-Do List
April

_____

_____

_____

_____

_____

_____

_____

_____

_____

_____

_____

Journal
April

_____

_____

_____

_____

_____

_____

_____

_____

_____

_____

_____

To-Do List
May

_____

_____

_____

_____

_____

_____

_____

_____

_____

_____

_____

Journal
May

_____

_____

_____

_____

_____

_____

_____

_____

_____

_____

_____

To-Do List
June

_____

_____

_____

_____

_____

_____

_____

_____

_____

_____

Journal
June

_____

_____

_____

_____

_____

_____

_____

_____

_____

_____

To-Do List
July

_____

_____

_____

_____

_____

_____

_____

_____

_____

_____

_____

Journal
July

_____

_____

_____

_____

_____

_____

_____

_____

_____

_____

_____

My Teenager's Third Year in High School

To-Do List

August

_____

_____

_____

_____

_____

_____

_____

_____

_____

_____

_____

Journal

August

_____

_____

_____

_____

_____

_____

_____

_____

_____

_____

_____

To-Do List
September

_____

_____

_____

_____

_____

_____

_____

_____

_____

_____

_____

Journal
September

_____

_____

_____

_____

_____

_____

_____

_____

_____

_____

_____

To-Do List
October

_____

_____

_____

_____

_____

_____

_____

_____

_____

_____

_____

Journal
October

_____

_____

_____

_____

_____

_____

_____

_____

_____

_____

_____

To-Do List
November

_____

_____

_____

_____

_____

_____

_____

_____

_____

_____

_____

Journal
November

_____

_____

_____

_____

_____

_____

_____

_____

_____

_____

_____

To-Do List
December

_____

_____

_____

_____

_____

_____

_____

_____

_____

_____

_____

Journal
December

_____

_____

_____

_____

_____

_____

_____

_____

_____

_____

_____

_____

To-Do List
January

_____

_____

_____

_____

_____

_____

_____

_____

_____

_____

Journal
January

_____

_____

_____

_____

_____

_____

_____

_____

_____

_____

To-Do List
February

_____

_____

_____

_____

_____

_____

_____

_____

_____

_____

_____

_____

Journal
February

_____

_____

_____

_____

_____

_____

_____

_____

_____

_____

_____

_____

_____

To-Do List
March

_____

_____

_____

_____

_____

_____

_____

_____

_____

_____

Journal
March

_____

_____

_____

_____

_____

_____

_____

_____

_____

_____

_____

_____

To-Do List
April

_____
_____
_____
_____
_____
_____
_____
_____
_____
_____
_____
_____

Journal
April

_____
_____
_____
_____
_____
_____
_____
_____
_____
_____
_____
_____

To-Do List
May

_____

_____

_____

_____

_____

_____

_____

_____

_____

_____

_____

Journal
May

_____

_____

_____

_____

_____

_____

_____

_____

_____

_____

_____

To-Do List
June

_____

_____

_____

_____

_____

_____

_____

_____

_____

_____

_____

Journal
June

_____

_____

_____

_____

_____

_____

_____

_____

_____

_____

_____

_____

To-Do List
July

_____

_____

_____

_____

_____

_____

_____

_____

_____

_____

Journal
July

_____

_____

_____

_____

_____

_____

_____

_____

_____

_____

My Teenager's Fourth Year in High School

To-Do List

August

_____

_____

_____

_____

_____

_____

_____

_____

_____

_____

_____

Journal

August

_____

_____

_____

_____

_____

_____

_____

_____

_____

_____

_____

To-Do List
September

_____

_____

_____

_____

_____

_____

_____

_____

_____

_____

_____

Journal
September

_____

_____

_____

_____

_____

_____

_____

_____

_____

_____

_____

_____

To-Do List
October

_____

_____

_____

_____

_____

_____

_____

_____

_____

_____

Journal
October

_____

_____

_____

_____

_____

_____

_____

_____

_____

_____

_____

To-Do List
November

_____

_____

_____

_____

_____

_____

_____

_____

_____

_____

_____

Journal
November

_____

_____

_____

_____

_____

_____

_____

_____

_____

_____

_____

To-Do List
December

_____

_____

_____

_____

_____

_____

_____

_____

_____

_____

_____

Journal
December

_____

_____

_____

_____

_____

_____

_____

_____

_____

_____

_____

To-Do List
January

_____
_____
_____
_____
_____
_____
_____
_____
_____
_____
_____

Journal
January

_____
_____
_____
_____
_____
_____
_____
_____
_____
_____
_____
_____

To-Do List
February

_____
_____
_____
_____
_____
_____
_____
_____
_____
_____
_____
_____

Journal
February

_____
_____
_____
_____
_____
_____
_____
_____
_____
_____
_____
_____

To-Do List
March

_____

_____

_____

_____

_____

_____

_____

_____

_____

_____

_____

Journal
March

_____

_____

_____

_____

_____

_____

_____

_____

_____

_____

_____

To-Do List
April

_____
_____
_____
_____
_____
_____
_____
_____
_____
_____
_____
_____

Journal
April

_____
_____
_____
_____
_____
_____
_____
_____
_____
_____
_____
_____

To-Do List
May

_____

_____

_____

_____

_____

_____

_____

_____

_____

_____

_____

_____

Journal
May

_____

_____

_____

_____

_____

_____

_____

_____

_____

_____

_____

To-Do List
June

_____

_____

_____

_____

_____

_____

_____

_____

_____

_____

_____

Journal
June

_____

_____

_____

_____

_____

_____

_____

_____

_____

_____

_____

To-Do List
July

_____

_____

_____

_____

_____

_____

_____

_____

_____

_____

_____

Journal
July

_____

_____

_____

_____

_____

_____

_____

_____

_____

_____

_____

About the Author

Betty McGee is currently working as a Community Coordinator Program Assistant for the Oakland Unified School District. She assists students who are in an "at risk" situation of failing to complete their basic education. These are over-aged and underachieving middle and high school students.

For nearly a decade she has given special presentations to parents and educators on the importance of parent involvement at the high school level at the Annual California Dropout Prevention Conference. She has also given presentations on parent involvement at the National Dropout Prevention Conference and the National High School Association Conference.

Betty has received recognition from the California Department of Education for the most comprehensive parent training, and for being one of the most valuable Outreach Consultants.

She is a graduate of John F. Kennedy University.

This book is available through iUniverse, Inc. at there web site www.iuniverse.com. It can also be ordered through all major book resellers on line.

CPSIA information can be obtained
at www.ICGtesting.com
Printed in the USA
LVHW031801120421
684240LV00004B/663